I dedicate this book to all children suffering in silence. My hope is that all parents, teachers, treatment professionals and others, who are touched by our children's silence, learn about Selective Mutism so that our children can find their voices.

Dr. Elisa Shipon-Blum

Selective Mutism Anxiety Research & Treatment Center Publishing
(SMart Center) Philadelphia, Pennsylvania
First published 2001, Revised edition 2003, Reprinted and revised July 2007
Copyright Rev. 2012 by Dr. Elisa Shipon-Blum

All Rights Reserved. No Part of this publication may be reproduced, stored in a retrieval system or transmitted, in any form, or by any means, electronic, mechanical, photocopying, recording or otherwise, without the permission of the publisher and author.

What is Selective Mutism?

"Selective Mutism is a complex **childhood anxiety disorder** characterized by a child's *inability* to speak in select social settings, such as school. These children are able to talk quite normally in settings where they are comfortable, secure and relaxed."

In an attempt to answer, '*What is Selective Mutism?*' I have recited a variety of textbook and medical terms, including the DSM-IV criteria, countless times. I have even shown photographs and short videos of children with Selective Mutism. However, the words and pictures used to describe Selective Mutism barely touch the surface of the true meaning of this childhood anxiety disorder that rids a child silent. One of the best ways to describe a child with *Selective Mutism* is to share the following poem with you.

What is Selective Mutism?

It is a beautiful little 4 yr old girl who loves to talk to her dolls…but she cannot speak a word outside the home…

It is an adorable 6 yr old boy who runs around boisterously in his backyard …but stands expressionless, staring into space, when he enters his classroom…

It is an 11 yr. old little girl who sings and writes beautiful songs at home…but cannot verbalize a sound to her teachers and classmates…

It is a 15 yr old boy who loves computers, roughhousing and joking with his best buddy… but is now cyber schooled because he cannot function within school.

It is a sensitive and perceptive little 5 yr old girl, who tells her parents all the exciting and fun things she wants to do at her birthday party… but has never spoken a word to anyone outside the home…

It is a comical 6 yr old girl, who dances and sings in the entertainment room, while her family proudly watches on… but stands motionless, and cannot utter a sound when her class rehearses for the school musical…

It is a 9 yr old boy cheering loudly and intensely as he watches his favorite hockey team score a goal… but sits alone at a party and sadly turns away when another child approaches him…

It is an artistic 7-year-old girl, who prides herself on talking about her artwork to her family and two best friends… but cannot talk to these friends at school…

What is Selective Mutism?   It is a child *suffering in silence*

Dr. Elisa Shipon-Blum

"Understanding Katie is dedicated to my beautiful daughter, Sophia, who has always had so much to say and is now able to say it. "

Dr Elisa Shipon-Blum

Introduction

'Understanding Katie' is a story about a little girl who suffers from Selective Mutism. She is a 'typical' child with Selective Mutism and is among the more than 90% of Selectively Mute children who also suffer from social anxiety.

'Understanding Katie' is meant for:

- Parents, teachers, clinicians and other individuals who are interested in *understanding* what a child with Selective Mutism endures emotionally, psychologically and physically during a typical day and at the same time, would like to learn various tactics/techniques to help the child suffering 'silently.'

- Older children/teens who would like to understand more about the disorder they suffer from. Most children with SM feel alone and isolated within their silence. In their minds, the whole world seems to be able to 'get the words out' and communicate with ease. This is quite a debilitating feeling when something as easy as 'speaking' is virtually impossible for them when in social situations, such as school. What is often more perplexing to these children is why 'the words DO come out' when they are at home and comfortable, yet 'do not come out' in other settings. 'Understanding Katie' allows children/teens suffering from the disorder to realize that they are NOT alone and that there are others out there who feel just as they do.

Not only do children with SM suffer in silence, but family members suffer as well. Parents are often bewildered and unsure of why their child cannot speak. Frustration, anger, confusion, guilt and desperation are just some of the emotions that parents feel.

Teachers often misinterpret mutism and frequently do not understand how to help the silent child. Thoughts that go through a teacher's mind are: Should they push the child? Bribe the child? Or just let them be? Why can't I get this child to speak? What am I doing wrong that this child is still not speaking? Is this child being oppositional and/or trying to get attention? What can I do to help and where can I find out more information to learn about reasons for the child's silence?

This guide is meant to supplement the story book, 'Understanding Katie,' in order to help others understand Katie's feelings, explain Katie's actions, and to introduce tactics that can be used in order to help offer support to the child with SM in times of stress and frustration. By reading 'Understanding Katie,' adults involved in the life of a child with Selective Mutism and social anxiety will hopefully begin to comprehend how this child feels and perhaps learn productive ways in which to help.

For individuals learning about Selective Mutism, there are certain important concepts to understand. Before we can discuss the events within *Understanding Katie*, individuals need to 'SEE' SM as a true <u>Social communication anxiety disorder.</u>

Treatment should never be geared towards getting the child to speak immediately but helping the child progress in a step-wise fashion to minimize anxiety, build self- esteem and to increase social confidence and communication in social settings.

Treatment should be focused on the **WHOLE CHILD, not merely on mutism.**

The child's anxiety level in a given situation determines his/her ability to socialize and communicate at that time. The more comfortable, the easier it is to engage and ultimately, communicate. The less comfortable and the more a child feels an expectation for speech and communication, the more anxious and difficult it is for the child to engage and communicate.

The **Selective Mutism--Stages of Social Communication Comfort Scale©** and the **Social Communication Bridge®** at the end of this guide, clearly demonstrate the various stages that a child with Selective Mutism experiences in his/her progression from mutism→speaking.

Some children, especially younger children, may 'skip' through some stages (especially if medication is used!) but for the majority, knowing these stages exist helps clinicians, parents and teachers understand 'where' the child is in terms of communication anxiety from one setting to the next and then plan realistic treatment goals.

Also, understanding that a child can CHANGE communicatively from setting to setting and from person to person makes understanding Selective Mutism that much easier. I.e. the typical child with Selective Mutism may be able to respond and initiate verbally to one person in one location (home!), yet become mute and barely communicative in another setting (school, birthday party, etc). Perhaps he/she can chat nonstop with an aunt or uncle at a family function, yet become mute, and able to communicate via nonverbal means when he/she sees this same relative the very next day! This can be quite confusing and frustrating unless there is a clear understanding that communication abilities changed due to the change in the child's anxiety level.

In order to know where on the SM-SCCS© and the Social Communication Bridge® a child falls in his/her social communication anxiety a treating professional must assess different locations and then determine the child's comfort in communication in these settings. In other words, the treating professional must KNOW how a child FEELS and his/her baseline level of communication from one setting to the next in order to help the child progress from one stage to the next.

How can a treating professional, parent or teacher KNOW how the child feels in terms of their feelings of anxiety??? Knowing the answer to this question is one of the most important aspects to helping the child overcome his/her anxiety!

First and foremost, the child must UNDERSTAND his/her anxiety disorder. The child must **acknowledge** that he/she has difficulty 'getting the words out' and communicating and must be able to **assess** his/her feelings. In other words, a child cannot overcome something that they are not aware of!

So often, parents insist that they do not want their child to KNOW that he/she has "Selective Mutism" Many parents do not want their child to 'think' that something might be 'wrong' or that he/she may be *different than other children.* A question I ask in reference to this is; doesn't a parent know that a child KNOWS something is 'wrong?' Everyone else seems to be able to speak when spoken to and initiate play with other children, yet this child cannot. Wouldn't it make sense to help explain to the child that you (as a parent, teacher, etc) understand it is hard for him/her to 'get the words out' in certain places?

For older children, knowing there is a term for their awkward silence is a huge relief! Obviously for younger children, using the words, 'Selective Mutism,' may not be comprehended easily, but using phrases such as: 'Having a tough time getting the words out;' 'When the words get stuck;' and 'Feeling scared,' are realistic ways to help EXPLAIN reasons why *the words don't come out.*

Having worked with children with Selective Mutism and social anxiety throughout the years, I can tell you with certainty that the majority of children feel **scared** and **uncomfortable** and it can be **hard** to getting the words out. I can therefore guide parents/clinicians/teachers, etc., to make this assumption with most children suffering with Selective Mutism.

YES, many children will deny their scared or uncomfortable feelings and it will take time to acknowledge their 'inability', but working with a treating professional who can help the child ACKNOWEGE then ASSESS his/her feelings of anxiety is CRUCIAL and until this can be accomplished, progress will be greatly limited.

Therefore, children with Selective Mutism must learn to assess feelings of anxiety. For most, using simple feelings charts with ratings between 0→5 usually suffice. Feelings of 'scaredness,' 'difficulty' or 'uncomfortableness' should be determined in a variety of social settings and with a variety of people. Feelings of 5/5 are the most 'scary/uncomfortable/difficult' where as 0/5 is feelings of ease and comfort. For the majority, being at home is a 0/5 and being in a large group setting is a 5/5! Obviously, there are points in-between. Feelings vary from location to location and from person to person.

For younger children or children whom are having difficulty gauging their feelings between 0→5, I recommend using 3,2,1,0 as number terms to describe their anxious feelings. 3 is 'really scary/hard; 2 is medium scary/hard; 1 is 'little bit' scary/hard and 0 is easy. Since each child is an individual, determining how the child relates to his/her inability to speak/communicate is important. The child must understand. Some interpret mutism as 'hard to get the words out,' 'feeling scared or nervous.' Focusing on the word, 'talk' is not recommended. For so long, children interpret 'talk' as something that they CANNOT do, but the whole world can do and the whole world wants them to do! Using the term, 'talk' has been negatively reinforced due to constant attention, and therefore elicits tremendous anxiety in many children.

In addition to understanding the SM-SCCS© and the Social Communication Bridge® there are a variety of terms that repeat themselves throughout this guide.

Desensitization: This is a common behavioral technique used to gradually and purposefully help a child 'get used to' an anxiety-producing situation. This is accomplished by creating a list of such scenes in order of increasing anxiety. Then, over time, expose a child starting with the least anxiety-provoking situation to build tolerance and comfort to be able to accomplish more difficult tasks.

Distraction: The art of using distraction is a known therapeutic technique to help our anxious children focus attention away from their worries/fears/concerns. Using humor, 'games' and other activities are the methods I have used in my practice. Therefore, distraction is created by purposefully involving a child in an activity, bringing up interesting topics of conversation, etc to remove their attention to often stress induced stimuli. Distraction is used as a tactic in breaking the pattern of anxiety for our children.

Silent goals and **child-directed goals:** GOAL planning is crucial to a child's treatment plan.

- For our younger children, usually preschoolers and early elementary aged children (until about 6 yrs. old) many of the goals are silent goals. This means goals are planned between the treating professional/parent/teacher to enable for comfort. Purposeful tactics are done to help the child progress without making the child aware of the purpose. I.e. planning play dates with other children, parent spending time in the school to help build comfort. It is important to note that for the majority of our precious children, they are often quite stubborn, assertive and strong-willed at times. As a result, planning 'goals' for them to do is often futile and does not work well. I recommend calling goals, 'games.' Games are associated with 'fun' and our children often do not feel threatened by this approach.

- Child-directed goals are where the child works with the treating professional and together determines the next logical step in the treatment plan. I have learned to realize that *feelings of control* are necessary for our children to have in their treatment process. Therefore, child-directed goals, where the child assesses their feelings to a particular tactic, or about a particular situation, helps with the development of inner feelings of control, and hence, progression of treatment by having specific goals to move forward communicatively.

Goal charts are used to keep track of accomplishments. Stickers, tallies or simple marks on the chart are visual confirmation of success. Goals/Games are carefully planned to enable for minimal feelings of anxiety and the development of confidence and feelings of accomplishment!

Positive reinforcement is used to *reward* a child for a particular goal. Incentives or 'rewards' are often needed to help inspire, encourage and 'gently nudge' our children to perform their necessary goals (tactics and techniques). For some children, especially younger children, receiving a sticker may be just enough to satisfy them. However, for the majority of children, receiving a sticker eventually becomes 'no big deal.' From working with so many children, experience dictates that the best rewards are **privileges** since toys or small gifts lose their effectiveness quickly. How many dollar store gifts can a child receive? Privileges are very real and tangible. Every child knows what it feels like to go out for ice cream, rent a movie, have a friend sleep over or stay up an extra 15 minutes. As you will see in the story, stickers represent a 'bigger reward.' Therefore as children get a bit older, it is not the sticker itself that excites our children, but what the sticker represents! Along with stickers, there are a variety of examples that can be used for positive reinforcement.

- Tokens, play coins, actual money, tallies, vouchers, etc.

For every 5-10 stickers, tokens, etc the child receives a prize or privilege.

There are many who would say that rewards are similar to bribes. If one wants to look at it this way, then they are unfortunately taking the wrong approach. Just like an adult goes to work and gets paid at the end of the week, a child needs to perform their goals or 'GAMES' (to make progress!). Positive reinforcement is a proven successful method to help the child feel good and receive recognition for a 'job well done.' Most of our children need some 'help' and encouragement to perform their goals or 'games;' hence, positive reinforcement.

Preparation and allowing for more 'warm-up' time': Key to understanding our anxious children is knowing that they need more time and preparation than other children to changes in routines or partaking in social events. In addition, our children need more time to feel comfortable or to become 'adjusted' to a social situation. Therefore, if a parent/teacher knows there will be a change in routine or unexpected social event, the child should be prepared early for an event/change and enabled adequate warm up time when they first arrive at an event. Parents/teachers should minimize initial expectations and understand that saying hello, goodbye, and thank-you or perhaps nonverbally communicating will take our children 'time.'

Need for **control:** Are children with Selective Mutism purposely being mute in order to control others and is mutism a manifestation of opposition and defiance? Many treating professionals, teachers and parents would say that our children are 'oppositional' and are purposely trying to control a situation by not speaking. That since the child CAN speak, that he/she is purposefully choosing to be mute. Some say it is a form of CONTROL and it is a way to get attention. I do not see mutism this way at all. YES, mutism is a form of control, but not in a purposeful vindictive manner, but as a result of anxiety and feelings of being out of control.

Individuals who suffer from anxiety often feel out of control. In order to feel less anxious, an individual tries to maintain inner control. Just as sufferers of obsessive-compulsive disorder perform rituals in order to gain inner control over their obsessions, children with Selective Mutism have developed MUTISM as means of maintaining inner control by avoiding anxious feelings brought on by 'speaking.' Their difficulty communicating is stressful and elicits scared and uncomfortable feelings. In order to **control** these feelings mutism and avoidance is created. This is a subconscious event not a purposeful event. When others consistently bring up mutism, and question the child 'why' speaking is not occurring, reinforcement and continual anxiety results. For some children, they become defensive, frustrated and increasingly more avoidant. This is where the oppositional tendencies surface.

I can see the 'oppositional tendencies' in some of our children. But what I believe is that our children are unable to verbalize and become frustrated as well as defensive. Parents, teachers and treating professionals often ask, beg, bribe and perhaps threaten a child to speak. If the child is unable to do so, what will result? Inner frustration and avoidance will result. Mutism is therefore being negatively reinforced.

For treating professionals who view SM as a form of opposition and purposeful control, I am certain their track record in helping a child overcome their silence is poor.

Children with Selective Mutism are not choosing to be mute and they are NO refusing to speak. They are merely trying to avoid anxious feelings and have therefore created a maladaptive method of coping.

VERBAL INTERMEDIARY® is important to understand. This term is used often within this guide. A Verbal Intermediary® is a person or object (I.E stuffed animal, finger puppet, etc) that can HELP transfer speaking INTO an environment and to a particular person.

As the SM-SCCS© and the Social Communication Bridge® clearly demonstrates, to progress from Stage 1 (nonverbal) → Stage 3 (verbal) one needs a method of transferring speaking. This is the Verbal Intermediary® and/or Sounds (such as the Ritual Sound Approach®) and/or augmentative devices

For some children, who have built comfort with another child or children, speaking or whispering might spontaneously occur over time; however, for most, who are nonverbal in school and other social settings but can speak or whisper to someone in that setting, the Verbal Intermediary® enables for verbalization to expand to others.

Before I begin with the guide I recommend that you first read 'Understanding Katie' alone, without your child/student. Think about the story. Think about what Katie is feeling, why she may be feeling the way she does and how the mother, teacher and others handle Katie's difficulty communicating.

Then, after you have formulated your thoughts, read through the following guide. My hope is that after you read it, much of the information presented will bring *light* to your ideas, thoughts and conclusions. Perhaps you will now have a different perspective on a child with Selective Mutism.

THE STORY

As the story begins, Katie's alarm clock goes off. However, Katie remains in bed, not wanting to get up. Why?

As Katie lies in bed she is anticipating her day at school. Katie has social anxiety and Selective Mutism. Children with social anxiety feel an array of anxious feelings prior to various social encounters. Headaches, nausea, stomachaches, joint pain, and even vomiting and diarrhea can occur prior to a social situation for the anxious individual. This first page is describing just that.

Mom enters the room and sees that Katie is not making much progress getting out of bed. This scenario is all too typical for our anxious children who learn to *'avoid'* when feeling anxious over social encounters and social expectations. *Hesitancy*, *procrastination* and *withdrawal* are all common manifestations of 'avoiding' anxiety. In Katie's situation, she is subconsciously avoiding going to school.

Interestingly enough, some mornings are tougher for Katie than other mornings. This particular morning is a bit more difficult than other mornings. We will learn more about this later as to why this is the case.

Since Mom cannot change the situation that Katie has to go to school, she uses a variety of learned tactics to help Katie begin to function and overcome some of her anxious feelings.

First and foremost, Mom comes into Katie's room with a smile. She listens to Katie's complaints and then reassures Katie (whose physical symptoms are very real) that she feels like this most mornings and will be ok. Special hugs and kisses help Katie by reassuring her that it is OKAY to feel as she does and Mom is there for her. This is crucial for the anxious child.

Mom then tries to **distract** Katie and at the same time provides **positive reinforcement** for her to get up, dressed and down for breakfast. Playing a game with a young child is often productive!

What better way to get Katie to get dressed than to distract her with a fun and happy game? Then, to provide a reward for doing this sets the right mood for a more productive morning!

Other tactics that could be used with young children are:

- Covering your eyes while they get dressed
- Racing the child to get dressed
- Providing an 'extra' reward if they are up and dressed prior to your arriving in the room.

For the older anxious child, more creativity and 'hand holding' is often necessary to encourage productivity.

If getting up in the morning is a common difficult situation, the child's treating professional should help parents with methods to alleviate anxiety in the morning as well as incorporate 'morning dilemmas' into the overall treatment plan by providing realistic goals/games for the child. I.e. Goals with positive reinforcement for Katie should be planned and added to her goal chart! She can then check off or add her sticker each and every morning that the goal is accomplished!

This concept should be transferred to other difficult or anxiety-producing situations that occur on a consistent basis. I.e. Bedtime and chores in an attempt to provide needed structure and routine, etc.

In regards to helping the anxious child cope, talking about expectations with children/teens is important. Anxious individuals do well with order, routine and consistency. Having an 'expectation chart' or goal/game chart for all age children is another way to make your expectations clear. For some children, who are interested in helping themselves overcome their anxiety, encouraging them to help with this chart is an excellent idea. For older children, making up their goals to add to the list enables for a feeling of control; something anxious individuals desperately need.

Another technique that Mom did was to have clothes set out the night before. This may seem trivial, but in reality it is not. Anxious children thrive on **order**, **routine** and **consistency**. It is not uncommon for many of our socially anxious children to want to wear certain outfits that they feel 'comfortable in,' hence, wear similar clothes day after day! They often like their hair the same way as well, simply because, for the majority of SM children, the last thing they want to do is bring attention to themselves.

Since Katie is obviously anxious in the morning, Mom does not want to create more anxiety by Katie having to contemplate outfits and worry over tiny details. Picking out an outfit the night before, while relaxed and comfortable, is a sure fire way to remove some added pressure in the mornings!

Mom obviously used a variety of positive techniques to help Katie in the morning.

Let's discuss what Mom may have done had she not understood Katie's anxiety.

1. Mom could have gone downstairs first, and then called up to Katie to tell her to get dressed and to come down for breakfast. This technique

would have only heightened Katie's anxiety as she lay in bed suffering with physical symptoms. Katie may have gone into a downward spiral of worry, as she lay alone in her room while Mom was downstairs calling for her.

2. Mom may have come into the room and gotten angry with Katie for not getting up and dressed when the alarm went off. Again, this would have caused worsening anxiety for Katie.

The above two scenarios would have obviously caused more distress for both Katie and Mom. As a result, both would have gotten more frustrated and upset, causing unnecessary distress first thing in the morning and prior to the start of school.

Mom used the following anxiety lowering techniques to help Katie COPE and deal with her morning routine:

- **Acceptance** (letting Katie know she understands and then offering kisses/hugs)
- **Distraction** (game play!)
- **Positive reinforcement** or reward (sticker for Katie's chart!)
- **Preparation** (encouraged Katie to pick out her clothes the night prior to avoid sudden frustration over what outfit she should wear to school)
- **Routine** (Mom encouraged Katie to get up, dressed, then come down for breakfast at a set time each day)

How did Katie cope with Mom's 'get up and get ready' techniques in the book?
EXCELLENT! Katie received the reassurance and acceptance that she needed. She was distracted enough by the game to get dressed, and she received a reward for her efforts! A WIN-WIN SITUATION all around!

How might Katie have acted if Mom had not been supportive and reassuring? Quite simply, Katie would have become more anxious and upset. Children often manifest anxiety behaviorally.

Tantrums, crying, inflexibility, acting stubborn and bossy are just some of the ways children manifest anxiety. This behavior, when misunderstood, often creates frustration for parents. Parents frequently get angry, the child gets more anxious, and a spiral effect is created which will only end in exhaustion and despair for all involved.

The story continues with Katie exclaiming happily that she is "DONE AND READY!"

Mom praises her efforts verbally (without bringing up how she felt earlier). Since Katie is obviously happy, there is no need to dwell on Katie's previous anxious behaviors.

Mom then rewards Katie with a sticker (**positive reinforcement**) to be placed on her **goal chart.**

In Katie's situation, 5 stickers enable her to go to the store to buy a magic trick.

Please note:
Stickers used with Katie are NEVER to get Katie to speak. They are meant to reward her for a job well done and praising of her efforts.

As the story continues, Katie has picked her sticker, placed it on her chart and eats breakfast happily.

Katie finishes breakfast only to hear her mother state that the bus is here. Immediately Katie begins to feel anxious. This is manifested by the sudden change in her facial expression and her reluctance in getting up. Anxiety is confirmed as she feels 'sharp pangs in her tummy.'

Again, Katie is reacting as a typical socially anxious child.
She fears social situations and her fears are manifested in a physical, emotional and/or behavioral manner.

Katie reiterates her feelings by realizing how she dislikes the 'feelings' she is getting. Actually, Katie's realization about her feelings is a POSITIVE step in the treatment process! For so many children, expressing and acknowledging feelings are extremely difficult. The fact that Katie can acknowledge her fears will ultimately help her know how to accommodate her feelings of anxiety and therefore give her a sense of inner **control.**

*** Working with a treating professional who can help the anxious child open up and express his/her feelings is KEY and crucial in the treatment process.*

Mom walks Katie to the bus. Obviously Katie has done this routine many times before because she has gotten to the point where she can separate rather well and get onto the bus despite her uncomfortable feelings. Katie sits alone feeling the physical manifestations of anxiety.

Sitting alone is very typical for socially anxious individuals. Sitting with others or being near others often elicits worsening anxious feelings. It is 'easier' physically to be alone than to endure the pain of trying to socialize.

However, what distinguishes social anxiety, and for the most part, Selective Mutism from other disorders is that individuals with social anxiety WANT to socialize with others; they just have great difficulty doing so. As Katie clearly mentions, she wants to be with the other children but just cannot. She sees the other children laughing and having fun and she cannot assert herself to interact or become involved with them due to scared or uncomfortable feelings. Katie makes it clear by her acknowledgement that even whispering elicits discomfort. Again, this is common among our anxious children.

What does Katie mean when she says she CAN'T be with the other children?
What she means is that she gets a severe feeling of anxiety. The feelings of FEAR that come over Katie are so intense that they become crippling and although she WANTS to participate with the others, the feelings incapacitate her and prevent her from doing so. She therefore is *avoiding* anxious feelings by sitting alone rather than enduring the scared feelings that result from social interaction.

The feelings of withdrawal and isolation that Katie endures repeat themselves over and over again in her daily life (and throughout the entire book).

** It should be noted that there are many children with social anxiety and Selective Mutism whom can sit with another child on the bus ride to school without feelings of fear. However, in the majority of cases, this is someone with whom the anxious child feels comfortable with and has either built a rapport or has sat with the same child time and time again. In addition, as the school year progresses, many anxious children will 'get used' to the school bus and perhaps develop a relationship with another child or begin to sit with less familiar children.

Since Katie is obviously uncomfortable, Mom should figure out ways to help ease Katie's anxiety. Perhaps finding out if there are any friends whom Katie has on the bus? Perhaps there is a child who is already on the bus that would love to sit with Katie, but since Katie goes to her seat alone, the other child thinks that Katie does not want to sit with her. Perhaps Mom can find out more about the students on the bus whom Katie would like to sit with. Perhaps Mom calls a friend of Katie's and explains to the Mom that Katie would like to sit with her daughter on the bus and find out if the other child is willing to save a seat for Katie. Mom can then direct Katie to the seat on the bus or tell Katie that a certain friend is saving a seat!

A challenge comes into play if the other child already has a friend she sits with on the bus or Katie does not know any children personally on the bus. When this occurs, suggestions would be for Katie to sit near the bus driver.

Ideally, prior to the beginning of school, parents should call the bus terminal and find out if there is a way to 'meet' the bus driver. Taking an hour of time, driving to the terminal, touring the bus and perhaps 'picking' a seat close to the bus driver is a wonderful way for our children to feel less anxious and more in control over the situation. Perhaps then, the bus driver can save that seat for Katie and her 'school bus buddy.'

Katie, and other children with Selective Mutism who have difficulty communicating, need a method, which will enable them to communicate in times of <u>emergency.</u>

Working this detail out, prior to the start of school is important. I.e., working with Katie to be able to hand a note to her bus driver in case of emergency should be practiced. This can be done where every morning she hands a note to him/her as she gets on the bus. Letting the bus driver know this will occur will help the driver initiate this interaction in the beginning since initiating is so difficult for most children with SM.

Katie should have a prewritten note that indicates common issues that may arise so that if she has to, she can hand this note to the driver. Obviously having a friend whom she feels comfortable with would be an ideal intermediary to help Katie verbalize and/or hand the note if need be. In the beginning stages, if Katie is 'too scared' to do this, Mom can go with Katie, and help her hand the note to the bus driver. Then, offer her a sticker (positive reinforcement) each time she does this. Again, this should be worked out so that Katie can feel safe and comfortable and know that if she needs someone to communicate to, there is someone there for her.

Arrival to school:

Upon arrival at school, Katie becomes more anxious. She does not look at others; she neither smiles nor looks comfortable. She is anxious and afraid. She is focused on "show and tell." Having to speak and answer questions is incredibly scary for individuals with social anxiety and Selective Mutism. The thought of speaking elicits such anxiety that Katie cannot even acknowledge that another child has bumped into her!

As mentioned in the beginning of this guide, Katie has a more difficult time getting up this particular morning. WHY? **It is Show and Tell morning!**

For the typical child with SM, Show and Tell can be quite debilitating, practicing in a small group of children perhaps 'showing' rather then 'telling' is recommended. Some children who are unable to show in a small group are encouraged to bring items to school and have a special location, i.e. the window sill to display their special item. For other children, who are comfortable in a group setting, but still nonverbal can stand with a friend who can 'tell' about their special item. Obviously the tactics are endless and depend on the individual child's communication and anxiety level.

Within the classroom, Katie stands alone as the other children laugh and are obviously having a good time. Katie is stiff, expressionless and seems to be staring into space.

This entire scenario is all too typical for children with Selective Mutism. Causes for these behaviors stem from within the brain and nervous system.

When SM children are confronted with fearful scenarios (MOST SOCIAL SITUATIONS), the nervous system is stimulated causing an array of bodily reactions. The body gets tense due to muscle tension. The blank, expressionless face that Katie exhibits is due to the skeletal muscle tension in her facial muscles. Understanding that the vocal cords are LINED with skeletal muscle, we can assume that perhaps Katie and other SM individuals actually have vocal cord paralysis when they are anxious causing their paralyzing silence!

This behavior, over time, becomes learned and ingrained. The 'frozen look' may dissipate, but the mutism persists. Therapy needs to focus on how to unlearn mute behavior by becoming more communicative, both nonverbally and verbally.

Within the classroom, while all of the children are mingling and having fun, Katie is UNABLE to join in due to her anxiety. She is therefore standing alone, next to Mrs. Ryan's desk.

It is incomprehensible to individuals who do not suffer from SM and social anxiety to understand this feeling of isolation. It is truly crippling and debilitating to the child.

How embarrassing to the child to stand there, alone, while others are having fun and interacting. Katie would like, nothing more, than to engage in play with the others, but just cannot.

Circle time is often one of the MOST difficult times of the day for our children. Not only is it in the beginning of the day, when most children are just *warming up*, but also it is an organized group activity where discussions and participation are expected. For the child with SM/social anxiety, this can feel like utter torture. Unfortunately for some, it can set the tone for a difficult and stressful day.

Mrs. Ryan is correct in going over to Katie and directing her to the group. Notice that the teacher is not making a 'scene' or calling over to Katie from across the room while seated at the circle.

During circle time, there is discussion about a magic trick. Katie is dreading being asked and she is dreading having to sit in the large group while the entire class joins together in figuring out the trick. Notice the body language that Katie is portraying. She is obviously suffering and turning inward as the class discussion goes on.

Everyone is taking turns with the magic trick, and Katie knows that she, too, will have to perform the trick. When it reaches her turn, another child comments that 'Katie does not talk.' Unfortunately, this scenario, where a student in the class will comment about mutism, is more common than we would like to admit. This student is not trying to hurt Katie, but merely stating a fact. Katie does NOT talk in school as far as he is concerned. Katie is mute.

Mrs. Ryan rescues Katie from her embarrassment and indicates rather strongly that Katie does indeed talk, but has a hard time 'getting the words out' in school.

Mrs. Ryan's explanation is an excellent comeback. First off, Katie was obviously not going to verbally defend herself and Mrs. Ryan knew that. She also wants the class to understand that Katie does speak; she is just having difficulty speaking in class. In addition, Mrs. Ryan did not focus on the word, "TALK." She used other words to describe how Katie feels.

"Talk" and "speak" are two words that elicit anxious feelings within our

children. WHY? Because those are the two words that the whole world seems to dwell on all day and every day. Changing the term helps redirect the focus away from the negative connotation that "talk" and "speak" seem to imply for the child suffering in silence.

Another way that Mrs. Ryan can address the issue of Katie's inability to 'get the word out' would be for her to ask each child in the class to think about what scares him/her the most. Offering suggestions to the students as examples help them think about what does scare them. Mrs. Ryan can then tell the class that Katie is perhaps not scared of the same things as they are, but is scared to 'get the words out' sometimes. This technique places 'feelings of scaredness' right back to the other children. This is important, simply because this is the ONLY way that others can begin to understand Katie's silence.

Katie's classmates should realize that EVERYONE is scared of something, and that talking is scary for Katie. Mrs. Ryan should inform the class that since Katie has a difficult time, they should not constantly ask Katie to speak or bring attention to her 'not speaking' because this only make Katie feel more uncomfortable. By doing this, Katie will hopefully not endure the constant pressures or expectations from others by comments that are made.

Back to Circle Time:

Since Katie cannot verbalize at this time, Mrs. Ryan suggests that Katie *show* the class how to perform the trick. Katie *hesitates* at first, but then performs the trick. Once she did the trick, Katie seemed to relax and began to smile as she, too, was proud of herself.

Quite a few interesting things happened here:

1. Mrs. Ryan did not pressure nor indicate to Katie that she expected her to explain the trick. She **ACCOMMODATED** Katie's inability to speak and allowed for Katie to complete the task at hand in a nonverbal way. This concept will probably need to carry over into many other aspects of Katie's education. Infact, the fact that a child with Selective Mutism can use alternative methods to COMMUNICATE should be mentioned in any IEP or 504 plan.

2. When Katie first took the magic trick she **HESITATED.** This is quite common among our anxious children. In fact, teachers, parents and clinicians should realize that if a child is very hesitant and unable to initiate, then his/her anxiety level is heightened. 'Hesitation' in response, whether verbally or nonverbally, should be a 'red flag' to teachers and parents that the child is anxious and they should try and find ways to help alleviate anxiety. Reasons for hesitation are not completely known, but theories focus on a slower cognitive processing speed when an individual is anxious.

This is crucial for individuals who are working with an anxious child. When asked a question or a task is to be performed, others might need to wait a bit for a response. This occurs with nonverbal and verbal communication.

* Individuals should not rush a child with Selective Mutism when a question is asked or a task needs to be performed. Give a child extra time to communicate. Depending upon the child's ability to communicate, the response may be either nonverbal or verbal.

** This concept can be applied to classroom activities or timed testing. When accommodating a child's needs, extra time may be needed to perform tasks or activities.

Hesitation and slowness to respond must be seen as a manifestation of anxiety.

Fortunately, in this scenario, Katie was able to perform the task. Mrs. Ryan knew that Katie is able to perform nonverbally during their classroom group discussions. Katie is working with her treating professional and during each session goals/games are planned. In the beginning of the year, Katie would sit motionless and was unable to respond to questioning nonverbally. She could neither point nor gesture comfortably; however, via various behavioral techniques (i.e., desensitization, modeling, fading techniques) Katie is NOW able to perform nonverbally within a larger group setting with less anxiety. Katie is moving up the communication scale!

If Katie could not communicate nonverbally, perhaps Mrs. Ryan would not have presented the Show and Tell magic trick the way she did. She would not have put Katie in the situation to potentially embarrass herself and cause heightened anxiety. Therefore, this is a prime example of why communication is necessary between treating professional, parents and teacher. Had Mrs. Ryan NOT known what Katie can and cannot handle, she would not know how to accommodate Katie's anxiety nor know the goals that Katie is working on to progress communicatively.

Katie WAS able to think clearly and perform the task at hand. She even SMILED (a clear indication that anxiety is not TOO HIGH). There are some SM children who are so anxious, that they would not have been able to 'initiate' and take the trick in order to perform the task. Many SM children may have sat there motionless and expressionless. These children are clearly severely anxious and the teacher, in the future, should find alternative means to accommodate the child's anxiety.

However, there are times that a child may NOT be able to perform a requested task. Unfortunately this is often viewed as oppositional or defiant behavior since responding to a request should be simple and effortless. However, anxious children are notorious for their inability to respond when feeling uncomfortable. As parents of children with SM know too well, when our children are severely anxious, they may shut down completely and freeze, turn away to avoid interaction or sit there staring. Teachers, treating professionals, family members and friends should understand that it is the anxiety the child feels that is causing their inability to respond, not defiance. However, this does not mean a child with SM cannot be defiant; however, the defiance is not CAUSING the mutism and an inability to communicate, the anxiety is.

Children with Selective Mutism and social anxiety experience anxiety within group settings. As a result, it is not surprising that many children may have a difficult time within the class setting. Therefore, it is often necessary to create accommodations to help the anxious child cope within the school setting.

Ways to help a child adjust to classroom expectations:

- Participate in SMALL group settings as much as possible. Perhaps at first, with only one or two children whom the child CHOOSES or is comfortable with. Gradually increase the group by adding one child at a time. Perhaps had Katie been TOO anxious, or was unable to TAKE THE TRICK, Mrs. Ryan could have mentioned to the group that Katie will try to perform the trick later on. Then, at another time, when she was with a small group, she could ask Katie if she wanted to try the trick.

- For some severely anxious children, it may take a parent in a more isolated setting, such as when few people are around in the classroom, to enable for enough comfort for the child to perform a task.

- Determine other ways for the child to communicate their information. If a child cannot communicate verbally, perhaps finding nonverbal means of communicating, such as writing, pointing, nodding, and signing. In some cases, whispering to someone else (Verbal Intermediary®!) so that the information can be communicated via another person.

In regard to the magic trick, executing the trick can be very hard for many children. It is a PERFORMANCE, something that some children have great difficulty with. Since the majority of children with Selective Mutism have social anxiety 'performance situations' can be very trying. However, Katie was able to do it! If she were working on positive reinforcement, she would receive an award, sticker, etc., for her EFFORTS.

After Katie performed the trick, she smiled, and felt proud of herself. She also realized that performing the trick was not as scary as she had imagined it would be.

Katie was 'cognitively' thinking to herself that 'it wasn't that hard.' She was able to assess her feelings and acknowledge her ability or inability to perform the trick!!!

In an ideal situation, when Katie was about to perform the trick, she would have been able to cognitively assess how 'afraid' or perhaps 'uncomfortable' she felt about doing the trick. Perhaps in her mind, on a scale of 1-5, performing the trick would be a "4". After having done the trick she would think to herself that was only a "2"!! It wasn't as hard as she thought it was going to be!!

This 'cognitive thinking' enables Katie to use a learned skill (and coping skill) to assess her feelings and then think about the result. The next time a similar situation occurs, she will realize that it won't be as scary! This is a form of cognitive behavioral therapy (CBT)

Katie's treating professional is obviously working with Katie on assessing and acknowledging her anxiety!

Recess

In the book, when it is time for recess and everyone lines up to go outside, Katie immediately becomes more anxious. Katie's sudden change in body language with her head down and looking expressionless should be evidence to her teacher that she is uncomfortable.

For the majority of children, recess is fun and something that they look forward to. For the anxious, socially phobic child, recess can be a NIGHTMARE! Katie cannot yet INITIATE interaction with other children; therefore recess is difficult for her.

For some children, who are able to INITIATE play and interaction, recess is less stressful, especially if the child has a friend or small group of friends.

In addition, recess is often a time where the socially anxious child feels that she may embarrass herself. Running, playing, climbing, etc., are all examples of times when she could fall or bring attention to herself.

Interestingly enough, the SWINGS are one of the SM child's favorite places to be during recess. Swinging is a way that child can participate without needing another person to 'play' with. Swinging is so peaceful and enjoyable. Little attention can be brought to Katie by swinging.

In Katie's case, a small group of children are requesting Katie to play with them. Like most young children with Selective Mutism, Katie is well liked.

Unlike children with other disorders, such as autism, children with SM are quite social and engaging (when comfortable). In the younger grades, peers are often very accepting of their 'silent' classmates. It is not uncommon for the teacher to state that the child with Selective Mutism is one of the most popular children in the class!

Katie is not quite comfortable today and is resisting interaction. Perhaps the Show and Tell activity caused an overall feeling of heightened anxiety. On other days, Katie is able to interact more freely with the other children.

Katie would like very much to play with the other children. However, the anxious feelings associated with interacting with the other children on the playground are causing Katie to withdraw from the situation. This is quite debilitating for Katie, certainly a self-esteem bomber. She certainly does not feel good about herself that she cannot initiate or even respond to the other girl's request for play.

Again, this scenario is all too typical for some of our children.

What could Mrs. Ryan do to help Katie feel more comfortable during recess?
--Mrs. Ryan could help Katie interact with the other children by bringing them together on the playground. Perhaps suggesting a joint game?
-- Katie could have a *recess buddy.* For most children, this is an excellent idea. Suggesting to Katie and perhaps another child that they 'hang out together' is a way to help interaction occur. This child should be someone who Katie is having play dates with and building a rapport with. In 'Understanding Katie,' Emma would be an ideal choice!
--Mrs. Ryan could talk with Katie during recess and suggest she sit with her or play near her. Obviously, this is more for a younger child who would like nothing more than to hang out with his/her teacher!

Back in the Classroom:

After recess, Mrs. Ryan is working alone with Katie to practice reading. Note Katie's initial behavior. She is looking down and somewhat expressionless. This is quite common for our more anxious children when there is an expectation placed upon them. Katie is mute and unable to read to Mrs. Ryan; however, Mrs. Ryan is clearly able to assess her comprehension and overall reading skills.

Since Katie is unable to initiate (Mrs. Ryan probably knows this!), Mrs. Ryan is NOT going to wait until Katie initiates interaction. She will ask Katie specific questions about the book and wait for her response. Katie CAN respond to Mrs. Ryan as evident throughout the book. However, responding, even nonverbally, often takes longer for Katie than for other children. Again, this is a manifestation of anxiety.

Katie pointed to the correct place in the book and Mrs. Ryan rewarded her for a job well done. 'Just pointing' is tough for Katie, perhaps a 3/5 or 5/5 in terms of feeling scared.

Mrs. Ryan stated that Katie smiled. This is evidence that Katie is feeling more relaxed and indeed proud of herself. Obviously, Katie has been **exposed** to this scenario before. Katie feels more comfortable as time goes on!

 **Note, in the beginning of the school year, Mom would spend time after class or before class with Mrs. Ryan and Katie to help her daughter feel more comfortable. Expectations in the beginning of the year for Katie to just nod and

point in response to her teacher's questioning were goals that Katie was working on.

Katie's anxiety level was accommodated by:
(1) Spending one on one time with just her teacher. Had Katie been expected to perform in a group, she may not have been able to respond. Recently, Katie had been working alone with Mrs. Ryan in the classroom. This was done after school when few people were around. At this point, Katie and Mrs. Ryan are 'doing the reading lesson' in the classroom, perhaps in a less populated area of the room. Assuming Katie's anxiety level is low enough, a next step might be for Katie to be working with Mrs. Ryan and perhaps a small group of children. Ideally, starting out with one or two children, then adding another child (or replacing) a child as comfort is established is recommended. These children should be the same children whom Katie is 'getting to know' outside of school. In some cases, having a parent present (especially for younger children) is recommended.

For some children, especially if a parent is unable to be present often, a classroom aid or 'wraparound' teacher to help Katie interact and communicate with others is an excellent idea. For some children, having an aide present a few times per week to work on necessary tactics is part of an IEP or 504 program.
(2) Being able to communicate her knowledge nonverbally.
(3) Giving Katie extra time to perform the requested task. In the book, Katie 'easily' pointed to the answer to the question. Her lack of hesitation is further evidence that Katie did not feel too anxious. This is positive!
(4) Praising Katie's efforts!

Other ways that Mrs. Ryan can assess Katie's reading level:

(1) Katie could tape her reading lesson on a videotape or audiotape.
** In my professional opinion, I do not see taping as a mode of treatment, but rather a way to accommodate a child's anxiety to enable schoolwork to be completed. I.e., Reading or performing a project via tape is a wonderful way for a teacher to assess learning. In addition, taping should NEVER be done if the child is highly resistant to this method. All that will be created is more anxiety!
(2) **Give Katie assignments where she can write her responses in a notebook**. Obviously Katie is a bit young for that, but for older children, communicating knowledge by drawing or writing is more than acceptable.
(3) **Using Verbal Intermediaries®**. This was not emphasized in the book, but verbal intermediaries are often used for the child in terms of progressing from nonverbal → verbal communication. As evidence in the upcoming page, Katie CAN speak to her mother within the school. Perhaps Katie, her mother and Mrs. Ryan can work together one day before or after school where Katie can whisper to her mother the answer to a question. Katie's mother will serve as the Verbal Intermediary® between Katie and Mrs. Ryan.
(4) **Asking a child to POINT in response to a question being asked.**
For children working on sounds, early reading, etc. teachers can ask questions:
-- Asking the child to point to particular words, sentences, etc in an attempt to assess letters/sounds, sight reading or early reading.

--Asking the child to point to letters that have a particular sound.

For older children a teacher can ask:
--About specific story content and ask the child to locate a particular segment within a book.
-- Ask yes or no questions about parts of the book where the child can nod or point (if the child is in the nonverbal stage) or <u>choice</u> questions (for children beginning in the verbal stage).

**KATIE should be an active participant in choosing what she can and cannot handle. If Katie is too anxious, there should be accommodations to help alleviate anxiety.

To date, I have yet to meet a child with SM who has FIBBED about being too scared. Quite the contrary, it is the resistant child who 'down plays' scared or uncomfortable feelings.

Therefore, trusting Katie's feelings of anxiety is crucial and key elements in helping Katie overcome her anxious feelings.

Katie's Mom arrives to the school:

At 3 o'clock, when all other children are leaving the school, Katie's mother enters the classroom. A few afternoons a week, Mom spends time with Katie within the school in an attempt to help Katie build comfort and to transfer speaking into the school environment. (Verbal Intermediary®!)

Mom asks Katie how her day was in an attempt to encourage verbalization within the class. However, Katie is not yet comfortable to speak since another child is still in the class. Katie is obviously elated by her day's accomplishments and is eager to share them with her mother! She is literally bursting at the seam with excitement! This is clearly evident by Katie's sudden change in 'body language' when it is just Mom and Katie within the classroom.

Is Katie being defiant or controlling because she 'waits' until the other individuals leave the room??
Absolutely not! This is classic and typical behavior for children with Selectively Mutism. Katie cannot verbalize comfortably with her mother with others present. Some of this is indeed 'learned' behavior that Katie cannot break free of just yet. However, she is clearly making progress communicatively and as she works with her treating professional, and as goals are worked on, Katie will eventually be communicating verbally in front of others.

This behavior, of not being able to talk with others present again, is all too familiar. This behavior will remain unless the child is actively working with an experienced professional to help him/her UNLEARN ingrained behaviors.

Therefore, SM is neither defiant nor controlling behavior, but maladaptive and avoidant behavior.

Within the classroom, Katie's relaxed body language, her ease in movements and obvious smiling and excitement is evidence that her mother's presence is comforting.

Mom is obviously very supportive of Katie. **Not once does Mom ask Katie whom she spoke to during the day or if she spoke at all. There is nothing mentioned about speaking!!**

Understanding and *accepting* Katie and <u>realizing</u> that she is too anxious to 'get the words' out during class and in front of others at this time enables Katie to feel less anxious. As a result, she is making wonderful progress. Both Mom and Mrs. Ryan *understand* that for Katie, just communicating nonverbally is an accomplishment!!

As time goes on and expectations are changed, Katie will begin to communicate more easily with others nonverbally and verbally. However, for now, the correct steps are being taken. We know this because of the progress Katie is making. In the beginning of school, Katie was practically noncommunicative. She is now responding nonverbally within the classroom to her teacher and most schoolmates and she is communicating verbally to her mother within the school when few people are around. This is progress!!

We can now see that a child with **Selective Mutism truly does have a communication anxiety.** In other words, depending on comfort, communication comfort varies.

If we were to refer to the SM-SCCS© and the Social Communication Bridge® at the end of this guide, we can see that Katie is in stage 1A with her teacher and classmates. She can point/nod and communicate nonverbally in response to a question. From the story, it seems that Katie is a 'typical' SM child who has great difficulty initiating nonverbally. She is probably not in stage 1B at the time of this story (initiating nonverbally with comfort)

So, with certainty we can assume that Katie is in stage 1A for most of her school day. Although she does hesitate with her responses in a group setting (as evident by her hesitation when doing the magic trick) she clearly responds with ease one on one with Mrs. Ryan during reading time. We do not see in this book her comfort with her peers nonverbally, but it is implied that she can reply to them nonverbally.

Katie is easily able to speak to Mom alone in the classroom. In addition, Katie is able to speak to Mom in the hallways too! Not only is Katie speaking, but also she is speaking in a normal tone!! As mentioned, just a few weeks prior, Katie was nonverbal in the school environment with Mom and was very hesitant with her responses. When Mom is present, and others are not present, Katie enters into Stage 3 (verbal stage)

It is important to understand that Katie's anxiety was causing her to be stifled in her ability to communicate. With careful planning using a variety of tactics & techniques, such as positive reinforcement and desensitization Katie is clearly making strides in communication and comfort.

This is progress!!

It should be noted; however, that there is no place that Katie has been pressured, pushed or bribed. As a result, with careful and purposeful planning, Katie has been making steady progress.

In the hallway with Mom:

On page 19 Mom and Katie are walking the halls. This section of the book is emphasizing a crucial aspect of a child's treatment plan to overcome Selective Mutism. Since Katie is unable to speak in school, she needs to 'see herself as a speaker' within the school environment in an attempt to 'unlearn' her present dysfunctional mute behavior and to realize that she CAN speak within school. This tactic is KEY for almost every child who suffers from Selective Mutism.

As mentioned throughout this supplement guide and demonstrated in the SM-SCCS© and Social Communication Bridge® within the introduction, in order to progress from nonverbal (stage1)→verbal (stage 3) there needs to be a way to transfer speaking into a particular environment; hence, Verbal Intermediary®. For the majority of children who are similar to Katie, a parent is an ideal choice!! What better person to help ease into verbalization that someone whom the child feels the most comfortable with? For Katie, Mom is the Verbal Intermediary®. Note: For other children who are verbalizing with a friend outside of school, using friends, as an intermediary, is an ideal choice.

Therefore, Mom's presence within the school at the end of the day is by no means a coincidence! This was planned and part of Katie's treatment plan!

In addition, this was not a random choice of tactics for Katie. As demonstrated on the SM-SCCS and the Social Communication Bridge® the normal and expected transition of communication goes from nonverbal→ verbal. Knowing where Katie falls within this scale is CRUCIAL in the goal planning process. I.e. Katie's treating professional has used Katie's feelings of anxiety, level of being scared or uncomfortable to assess her ability to perform this particular goal.

This tactic should be used with ALL children suffering from Selective Mutism/social anxiety. Not only does spending time alone with a parent or other individual whom the child is comfortable with **desensitize** a child to the school environment but allows comfort in communication to occur. As mentioned within the book, 'Understanding Katie,' there was a time where Katie could not speak to her mother in school. She would freeze and stand motionless when she was within the school environment.

Mom, therefore, spent time with Katie as a means of building comfort within the school. As time progressed and Katie became more and more comfortable, increase in communication occurred

As mentioned, the goal process is critical in helping our children progress forward. However, as mentioned in the beginning of this supplement guide, for younger children (preschoolers and early elementary students) this particular tactic is a silent goal and should NOT be used as means of 'expecting' the child to speak. The treating professional should encourage one on one time within the school without telling Katie she should speak to her mother when spoken to. If Katie felt she 'had to' speak, more anxiety would have been created.

Spending time alone, with a parent or an individual whom the child is comfortable with, over time, enables for AUTOMATIC increase in communication. Obviously the time to accomplish this feat varies from child to child and is dependent on their overall anxiety level.

The concept of helping to build communication comfort within school was also implemented with the classroom teacher. Mom, Katie and Mrs. Ryan spent a great deal of time within the classroom without others around. Mrs. Ryan would stay after school occasionally, would meet them early in the mornings, etc. so that Katie could build comfort with her teacher without classroom peers present. This was done consistently and often. For times when Mrs. Ryan was unable to meet with Katie before/after school, she would spend time with her during recess, lunch or snack time

Picking up Emma:

Mom picks up Emma for a play date (silent goal!). Crucial to helping our children is to encourage social interaction, one child at a time, in order to begin building a comfortable relationship. Ideally, having play dates at home is the way to begin!! Children are usually the most comfortable within their home environment. Therefore, the home is an ideal place to start building a social relationship with another child without the pressure of others around.

It is obvious that Katie is very comfortable with Emma. Not only is Katie communicating with ease, but also she is 'initiating' conversation (stage 3b). It should be noted, that a few months earlier, when Emma first came over to Katie's home, Katie communicated via responding via nonverbal means of communication. She pointed, nodded and gestured as she does in school, but she could not initiate nonverbally (Stage 1a). Mom or Dad planned the first few play dates at a park to help Katie feel less anxious. Going to a park, mall or other location where Katie did not have to focus on one on one play where the children would need to directly interact together, helped build initial comfort. Then, the next few play dates were planned at home. Mom baked cookies, set out crafts and helped the girls interact. She would ask questions that required answers to stimulate communication. Katie easily responded nonverbally and within a few play dates was talking directly to Mom in front of Emma. Within a short period of time, after Mom started the girls off with a game, Mom left the room and verbalization continued!

Mom is having play dates with other children as well. Katie presently has three friends whom she can speak to at home. Silent Goals are to merge these friends together during an upcoming play date!

Although Katie is quite verbal and comfortable with Emma at home, she is still mute with Emma at school. This is all too typical for our children who can be one way in one setting with one person, then completely different with that same person in another setting! Communication comfort changes by the environment our children are in as well as with the individuals whom they are with.

Is Katie's 'refusal' to speak to Emma in school a representation of defiant and controlling behavior?

Absolutely not!! Katie's' heightened anxiety within the school environment is preventing her from communicating verbally with Emma (and other children) evidenced by the playground scenario earlier in the book. Katie does not REFUSE to speak to Emma at school, but is truly unable to.

For young children, such as Emma, a situation where her friend can interact and speak freely to her in one place, then withdrawal and become mute in another is a difficult concept to comprehend.

Recommendations when a 'friend' is confused and asks why their friend 'doesn't talk' at school, but talks at home, should be explained in the following way:
--"Katie gets uncomfortable and 'scared' feelings at times when in school and when that happens, 'the words do not come out.' This is frustrating to Katie since she wants to be able to speak to you in school. When there are a lot of children around, lots of action going on, etc., it is harder for Katie. At home, Katie is comfortable and able to speak with you. Katie's inability to 'get the words out' can also happen in other places too, such as at parties, friends houses and when meeting new people. Just being Katie's friend and letting her know you care will help Katie feel better."
--By asking the other child to name something that scares him/her or is hard to do. Relating the other child's personal feelings to Katie's feelings of 'feeing scared' or 'having a difficult time' getting the words out is often enough explanation.

Emma happens to be an assertive child. She is outspoken and often does much of the talking for Katie. This is not as clear in Book 1, but will be evident in future Katie books.

Interestingly enough, **children with Selective Mutism tend to bond with the more assertive and chatty classroom children. WHY?** Quite simply these are the children whom INITIATE with our typically timid children. The outgoing children take charge!! This is often a relief for our children who cannot comfortably initiate!

In addition, outgoing children can do a lot of communicating for our children. It is not uncommon for the outgoing pal to do the talking for a child with Selective Mutism.

This brings up an important and often asked question:

Is it enabling if another child is speaking for the child with Selective Mutism?

Not necessarily. Depending on where the child is communicatively in terms of anxiety and their ability to communicate comfortably dictates whether enabling is occurring.

For example:
- If the child is minimally communicative with one friend in the classroom and can indicate via nonverbal means to that one individual, a friend speaking for him/her is appropriate. WHY? Because the child is communicating at the level that he/she is capable of at that time. However, if the child is in the verbal phase, able to answer various individuals in the class, then it is inappropriate for another child to whisper or talk for the child with Selective Mutism.
- As mentioned throughout this guidebook, transitioning from nonverbal to verbal communication often involves a Verbal Intermediary®. Therefore, if a child is questioned by someone whom he/she cannot speak to, but can whisper or talk through a friend (Verbal Intermediary®) as part of their treatment plan to progress communicatively, then the child is increasing their communication!
- Children, who are mute in various settings, rarely go from mutism to speaking. However, if a child is comfortable whispering and there is no progression of communication despite the child's 'ease' with whispering to a friend, then YES, whispering to a friend for months on end without progressing communicatively is indeed enabling.

**Under the guidance of a treating professional, goals/tactics that are implemented within the school setting (monitored and implemented via a team approach with the school team), the child should progress from nonverbal→verbal communication.

In 'Understanding Katie,' Katie is not yet speaking to her friend in class. Perhaps this is a goal that is being worked on!

However, Katie can obviously speak to Emma outside of the school environment. IE. In the car, at home, etc.

As part of Katie's treatment plan, there should be ways to help Katie transfer speaking with Emma INTO the school environment.

Katie's treating professional should encourage Mom to allow Katie and Emma to have a play date at the school! An ideal situation would be to begin the play date at home when speaking is occurring easily and effortlessly, and then transfer to the school playground. With few people present on the school grounds, speaking is most likely going to occur.

The school should be receptive to allowing MOM, Katie and Emma to spend time within the school environment without others around. Just as Mom does with Katie in the school!

The use of this tactic (transferring verbalization into the school by transferring play dates from home-→school) is an example of a silent goal for Katie.

Although not specifically mentioned in the book, Katie's mom was encouraged to go BACK to the school after picking up Emma for a play date.

Katie and her family:

In 'Understanding Katie,' Katie's family interacts and talks about her goals and accomplishments while eating dinner. It is clear that Katie's treatment process and goals are talked about positively and with enthusiasm. Katie WANTS to perform her goals and receive rewards. She is obviously very excited!

Is this scenario, does 'talking' about Katie's goals bring too much attention to Katie's mutism and issues at hand?

Absolutely NOT! In order for Katie to overcome her mutism and anxiety, she must understand and be an active participant in the entire process. She must be willing to help 'herself' and be involved in the goal setting.

In addition, the family is NOT talking about 'talking.' Her parents are not drilling her or asking her why she is not talking to her teacher or school mates, nor are they giving her rewards for speaking.

Attention is taken away from 'not talking' or 'talking' but emphasis is on goal accomplishments!

Too often, individuals focus on whether or not a child is speaking, who he/she is speaking to or not speaking to. This emphasis and attention to speaking is considered a **negative reinforcement** for mutism. The child's inability is focused on, which in turn, only creates more anxiety, hence persistence of mutism!

Back to the book:

The story concludes with Katie's bedtime.

Notoriously, Katie has had tantrums in the past, acted out and would become irate over bedtime. Katie's parents had a difficult time understanding why this occurred almost every night.

A fact: Anxious children usually have a difficult time with **bedtime.**

Going to bed can translate to:
(1) Separating from Mom/ Dad
(2) The 'scary' dark
(3) 'Difficulty falling asleep'- a common characteristic of anxiety!
(4) The thought of waking up early, alone and waiting for others to awake – early morning awakening is characteristic of anxiety.

To help with Katie's tendency to 'act out,' and procrastinate at bedtime, Mom **prepares** Katie in advance that bedtime is in five minutes. If she goes upstairs prior to the five minutes being up, she gets a reward (notice goal chart!) Mom could use a kitchen timer with a bell or alarm clock as a warning signal for Katie to know that it is bedtime.

One of Katie's goals is to go to bed at a certain time and to respond to her mother's request for getting ready for bed. We clearly see that Katie reacts positively to her mother's request. Katie is running up the stairs while Mom praises her positive behavior! Her mother then incorporates a bedtime **routine** that consists of story reading, talking about Katie's day and cuddling. **Frequency and consistency in routines help children feel 'in control' and hence, less fearful and anxious.**

Obviously, the disappearance of 'difficult night time' behaviors did not occur immediately, but after a period of time, maintaining a bedtime routine and talking with Katie about her worries/ fears and acknowledging her concerns, behaviors improved greatly.

Rewarding positive behavior (positive reinforcement) is important for our children. Bringing attention to negative behaviors only creates more tension and anxiety, lower self-confidence and frustration for all.

Focus should be:
**Reward positive behaviors and to bring little attention to negative behaviors. Results are: positive self-esteem, hence lower anxiety.

Common to children with Selective Mutism and other anxieties, is their need for **warning and preparation**. Most children do not do well with sudden changes or expectations.

Throughout the book we can look back and examine a few scenarios where warning and preparation may have helped or did help Katie cope and feel less anxious.
(1) During show and tell, Katie sat looking withdrawn and obviously anxious. She was unprepared for the magic trick. She was obviously uncomfortable. When it was her time to do the trick, she hesitated, but did perform the trick. Had Katie had preparation that she would be asked to perform a magic trick, perhaps she would have felt less anxious.

(2) Katie read to Mrs. Ryan. She seemed relaxed and was able to communicate nonverbally. Katie was prepared for reading with Mrs. Ryan. Three times per week she spends one on one time with Mrs. Ryan during class time. This is also an example of desensitization. For the entire school year, Katie has been spending time with Mrs. Ryan. In the beginning, Katie was minimally communicative with Mrs. Ryan. She could barely point/nod and was very hesitant with her responses. Over time, using a variety of tactics and techniques, she has become less anxious and more communicative.

(3) Bedtime. Mom preparing Katie to get ready for bed with a five-minute warning is fine and appropriate. Since bedtime is not Katie's favorite time of day, giving her warning and having an expectation is needed. Notice that Katie is distracted by her 'wanting' to please and receive another sticker, so, in some ways, she has become distracted to the point of 'forgetting' that bedtime is normally very anxiety provoking for her!

Warning and preparing our anxious children for even the slightest change in routine cannot be emphasized enough. The more our kids know and feel prepared, the less anxious they will feel.

The end of the book focuses on Katie spending time alone with Mom. This is their 'special time' each and every night. Mom often alternates with Dad where they spend time each evening cuddling with Katie. Together they talk about her day and she has an opportunity to 'express her feelings.

From information gathered at the Selective Mutism Anxiety Research and Treatment Center (Smart Center), many children with Selective Mutism have difficulty expressing their inner thoughts and concerns. However, for treatment to be positive and for a child to gain control over anxiety, expressing and coming to terms with difficulties is crucial and necessary.

At bedtime, while Mom snuggles with Katie, she is enabling Katie the opportunity to *open up* and express herself. Interestingly enough, Katie's ability to express her feelings was something that she needed to learn to do. For so long, Katie denied her anxiety and 'inability' to speak. She would turn her head, get upset and avoid discussing her mutism. Katie would often tell her parents that she did not want to speak, was not going to speak and did not care!

NO child wants to be mute. However, as time goes on, and a child is unable to do something that they want to do (in this case, speaking) a child will build a wall of defense. Something as easy as speaking is impossible. Words come easy at home, yet words get stuck in school! How **perpelexing**!

As mentioned, important in Katie's treatment plan is her ability to <u>acknowledge and assess</u> her inner feelings. This is actually the first step in the process of overcoming Selective Mutism (anxiety!). Therefore, Katie's treatment professional has worked with Katie and her parents to help her 'open up' and come to terms with her feelings. After a short time, her doctor realized that similar to other children with Selective Mutism, Katie often felt **scared** and 'the words were hard to come out' at school, at parties, in a restaurant, etc.

The beginnings of 'feeling in control' were accomplished when Katie could UNDERSTAND WHY she was unable to get the words out.

Katie's words got stuck because she felt SCARED. This made sense to Katie!

Since Katie realized WHY the words get stuck at times, she slowly began to open up about her difficulty. Infact, much of her oppositional comments began to dissipate. The wall of defense began to break down! So, now, at bedtime, instead of Mom asking questions about how she felt in school, etc. Katie often states her feelings. This experience of 'opening up' has enabled Mom and Katie to become closer than they were before treatment began. Nighttime is something that Mom cherishes so that she and Katie can snuggle up close and Katie can feel free and relaxed to let the words flow…

'Understanding Katie' is a book about a young girl who suffers in silence as so many children with Selective Mutism do. The book is a 'day in the life' of Katie and involves many different aspects of struggles and triumphs.

The key to Katie's progress is focusing on her social communication anxiety not her mutism. Speaking or not speaking should not be a focus for treatment.

WHY? Because the treatment of Selective Mutism involves so much more than 'just speaking!'

Treatment of Selective Mutism should focus on ways to help children gain control over their anxiety by helping them acknowledge and assess their scared and uncomfortable feelings when in an 'anxious' setting, build their self-esteem and help to increase their social confidence and communication. Treatment should NOT focus on getting a child to 'talk.' When treatment emphasis is on getting a child to 'talk' anxiety is heightened, and communication comfort is greatly limited.

A note from the author:

"This book was inspired by my experiences with my own child. My goal for this book, and the work that I do every day in helping children overcome their silence is for parents, teachers and treating professionals to understand that Selective Mutism is very real. Children truly suffer in silence. They need acceptance, understanding and patience from everyone involved in their life.

Although mutism is the most obvious symptom in our 'silent' children, understand that Selective Mutism is not about 'mutism,' but about difficulty and anxiety with social communication, hence SM Is a social communication anxiety disorder; hence, the evidence-based treatment, Social Communication Anxiety Treatment

(S-CAT)®. When seen and treated from a communication anxiety perspective, the prognosis for building necessary coping skills to combat anxiety is excellent."

Dr. E

ADDENDUM:

Below is Katie's goal chart for the week. Notice GOALS for communicating and goals for positive behaviors. Again, the treatment for Selective Mutism is MORE than just 'treating to speak.'

 * Goals for communicating are based on Katie's anxiety level. I.e., when asked if Katie will ask friend for play date, Katie graded feelings as 2/5. She therefore was prepared to do goal!

Katie's GOALS	Mon	Tues	Wed	Thurs	Fri	Sat	Sun
1 Get up/dressed in AM when alarm clock goes off!							
2 Spend time with Mom after school. Rate feelings before/after spend time in the hall.							
3 Do reading with Mrs. Ryan. Point/nod in response to question							
4 Do show and tell (can show) rate feelings before/after							
5 When at restaurant, whisper to mom (up-close) when giving order in front of waiter.							
6 Whisper to Mom in response to Mrs. Ryan's questions. Mom to repeat answer. (Alone in classroom)							
7 Invite Emma, Janet, Missy and Tara to have play date (Mom to make phone call, When friend gets on phone, Katie to talk with friends) grade feelings							
8 Hand note to Mrs. Ryan 2 times per day.							
9 clean room, put out clothes for night before							

10 Get ready for bed before 5 minute warning goes off						

SELECTIVE MUTISM-STAGES OF SOCIAL COMMUNICATION COMFORT SCALE ©

NON-COMMUNICATIVE -neither neither nonverbal nor verbal. NO social engagement.

0 - NO Responding, NO initiating
Child stands motionless (stiff body language), expressionless, averts eye gaze, appears 'frozen,' **MUTE**
OR
Seemingly IGNORES person while interacting or speaking to other(s). **MUTE towards others**

*For communication to occur, <u>Social Engagement</u> must occur

COMMUNICATIVE (Nonverbal and/or Verbal*)
*TO ADVANCE FROM ONE STAGE OF COMMUNICATION TO THE NEXT, INCREASING SOCIAL COMFORT NEEDS TO OCCUR.

STAGE 1 - Nonverbal Communication (NV)
1A Responding -pointing, nodding, writing, sign language, gesturing, use of 'objects' (e.g. whistles, bells, Non-voice augmentative device (e.g. communication boards/cards, symbols, photos)

1B Initiating -getting someone's attention via pointing, gesturing, writing, use of 'objects' to get attention (e.g. whistles, bells, Non-voice augmentative device (e.g. communication boards/cards, symbols, photos)

STAGE 2 - Transition into Verbal Communication (TV)

2A Responding -Via any <u>sounds,</u> (e.g. grunts, animal sounds, letter sounds, moans, etc.), Ritual Sound Approach RSA)® <u>Verbal Intermediary</u>® or Whisper Buddy; <u>Augmentative Device with sound,</u> (e.g. simple message switch, multiple voice message device, tape recorder, video, etc.)

2B Initiating -Getting someone's attention via any <u>sounds,</u> (e.g. grunts, animal sounds, letter sounds, moans, etc.), <u>Verbal Intermediary</u>® or Whisper Buddy; <u>Augmentative Device with sound,</u> (e.g. simple message switch, multiple voice message device, tape recorder, video, etc)

STAGE 3 - Verbal Communication (VC)

3A Responding – Approximate speech/direct speech (e.g. altered or made-up language, baby talk, reading/rehearsing script, soft whispering, speaking)

3B Initiating - Approximate speech/direct speech (e.g. altered or made-up language, baby talk, reading/rehearsing script, soft whispering, speaking)

Copyright © Dr. Elisa Shipon-Blum and SMart Center. www.selectivemutismcenter.org
Part of Social Communication Anxiety Therapy (S-CAT)®. Users to comply with copyright laws.

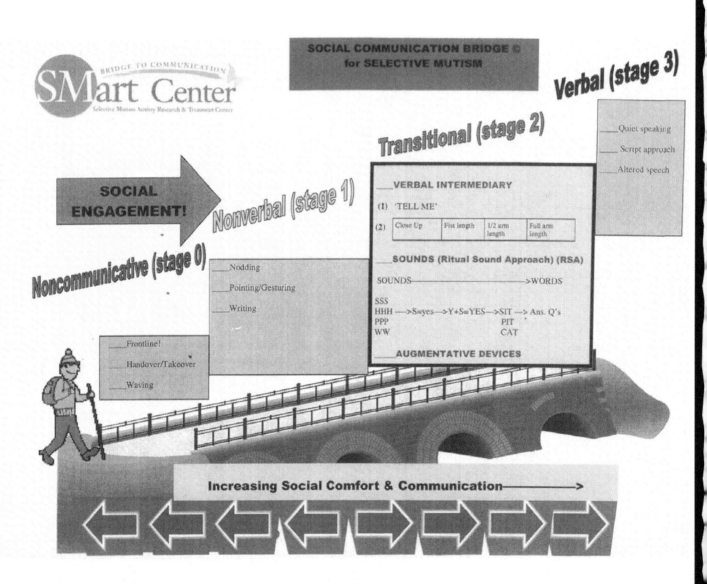

Copyright© Dr. Elisa Shipon-Blum and SMart Center. www.selectivemutismcenter.org
The Social Communication Bridge® Part of Social Communication Anxiety Therapy (S-CAT)®.
Users to comply with copyright laws.

The SMart Center offers and array of services and products related to Selective Mutism!

SMart Center contact information:
Director: Dr. Elisa Shipon-Blum
Web: www.selectivmutismcenter.org
Email: smartcenter@selectivemutismcenter.org
Phone: 215-887-5748 ~ **Fax:** 215-827-5722
Address: 505 Old York Rd. Jenkintown, PA 19046

Services:
--Evaluation & treatment services (using the evidenced-based Social Communication Anxiety Therapy (S-CAT)® for children 3-20 yrs. old via in-person, telephone and web-consults
--Ask the Doc consults for parents, treatment professionals and school staff seeking advice on case management, school recommendations and questions related to treatment.
-- School services: In-school child evaluations and ongoing consultation services, IEP and 504 development, staff trainings and school-based webinars
--Speech and Language evaluations and treatment for children with SM
--Professional workshops on-site and webinars!
--'Selective Mutism Conferences' around the country

Products: Available at the SMart Mart via www.selectivemutismcenter.org
--**Books**: Available as hard copies and E-Books:
Ideal Classroom Setting for the Selectively Mute Child
Easing School Jitters for the Selectively Mute Child
Understanding Katie (story book about a child with SM)
Supplemental Guide to 'Understanding Guide' for Parents, Professionals & Therapists
Unspoken Words; A Child's View of Selective Mutism.
--**DVD's:**
Selective Mutism; Socializing and Communicating in the Real World (~2 hrs.)
Medication in the Treatment of Selective Mutism (~2 hrs.)
Understanding and Treating Selective Mutism as a Social Communication Anxiety Disorder (~5 hrs.)
--*NEW!* **LIVE and Prerecorded Webinars!**

Limited offer! 20% discount to purchase more products at the SMart Mart!
Go to: http://selectivemutismcenter.org/products/products Use discount code: save20now

Made in the USA
Charleston, SC
06 December 2012